Editor
Karen Tam Froloff

Editor/Consultant
Dr. Ananda Gurage, PhD, D Lit

Managing Editor
Karen J. Goldfluss, M.S. Ed.

Editor-in-Chief
Sharon Coan, M.S. Ed.

Illustrator
Cover Artist

Art Coordinator
Kevin Barnes

Art Director
CJae Froshay

Imaging
James Edward Grace

Product Manager
Phil Garcia

Publishers
Rachelle Cracchiolo, M.S. Ed.
Mary Dupuy Smith, M.S. Ed.

EXPLORING WORLD BELIEFS
Buddhism

Author

Gabriel Arquilevich

Teacher Created Materials, Inc.
6421 Industry Way
Westminster, CA 92683
www.teachercreated.com
ISBN-0-7439-3683-3
©2002 Teacher Created Materials, Inc.
Made in U.S.A.

Table of Contents

Why Teach Religion?

If your students were asked what they know about Hinduism, Islam, Buddhism, Judaism, Sikhs, or Christianity, they might very well respond with a limited amount of information. Although they are impacted almost daily with information related directly or indirectly to religious issues, they often know little about the religions themselves or the lives of the great spiritual leaders.

Why has the study of religion been neglected? In the early 1960s, the Supreme Court declared state-sponsored religious activities within the public schools to be unconstitutional. However, the Court emphasized that learning about religion is essential. Despite the importance of religion in history and culture, most schools have traditionally kept a distance. Fortunately, this distance is being bridged.

As our world becomes more interdependent, there is a need to awaken to one another's spiritual heritage. Throughout history, the world has been shaped by people's religious beliefs. To teach history without religion is equivalent to teaching biology without reference to the human body. School boards across the nation now recognize this issue and have begun to advocate religious studies within the framework of history.

Religious studies foster tolerance. This is, perhaps, the most valuable lesson. Racism and stereotypes are born largely out of ignorance. How wonderful to give students the opportunity to listen to a Buddhist speaker or to visit a synagogue and ask questions of a rabbi. These kinds of direct contacts are invaluable.

Meeting Standards

The National Council for the Social Studies (NCSS) developed curriculum standards in the mid 1990s. These standards have since become widely used in districts and states as they determine essential knowledge and skills acquisition for students. At least two of the ten themes that constitute the social studies framework standards address the study of institutions, cultures, and beliefs. Theme I (Culture), for example, asks students to consider how belief systems, including religion, impact culture. Theme V (Individuals, Groups, and Institutions) challenges students to study the ways in which institutions and religions develop and how they influence (and are influenced by) individuals, groups, and cultures.

Within the NCSS framework, these themes are addressed for all students (early grades through high school). Therefore, support materials such as the books in this series, *Exploring World Beliefs*, are important resources for teachers to use as they work toward meeting standards in the classroom.

Introduction

Religions Originating in South Asia

Share with students the following information:

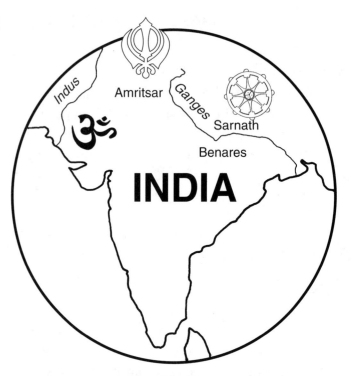

The Hindu, Buddhist, and Sikh religions originated in the South Asian subcontinent comprising India and Pakistan, beginning with Hinduism as early as 2000 BCE. These three religions differ from the Semitic faiths in some of their most basic beliefs. Hinduism, for example, is a polytheistic religion, meaning that Hindus may believe in various forms of God. (*Poly* means many, while *theism* means belief in God or gods.) Buddhists, on the other hand, do not necessarily believe in God at all. The Sikh religion, the youngest of these faiths, is monotheistic (believing in one God) like the Semitic faiths.

The Indus valley, nurtured by the Indus River, is the birthplace of Hinduism. The Buddha delivered his first sermon at the city of Sarnath near the sacred Hindu city of Banares. To the North is Amritsar, the spiritual center of the Sikh religion. As you can see, this area of the world was the starting point for many religions. Hindus number over 800 million worldwide and make up a large majority of the one billion population of the present day India. There are about 20 million Sikhs with about 80 percent living in India. Buddhism expanded into the rest of Asia to become the dominant faith in China, Japan, and many countries of South East Asia. In India, Buddhists are now a small minority.

About Date References

The abbreviations BCE, BC, AD, and CE are common terms used to reference time. (In this series, BCE and CE are used.) Some students may not be familiar with one or more of these terms. Use page 47 to introduce or review the abbreviations with students.

Suggestions for the Teacher

The books in this series present content that introduces students to several world beliefs. Various terms, phrases, and general content may, at times, be difficult for students to comprehend. It is suggested that segments containing intense factual content be read and discussed together. Have students keep a journal in which they outline important information and maintain a glossary of new terms and their meanings.

The Story of Buddha's Enlightenment

Buddhism began over 2,500 years ago. The foundation of Buddhism rests on the life of one teacher, an Indian prince named Siddhartha Gotama. Prince Siddhartha grew up in a small kingdom in northeast India, an area which now rests in Nepal. His father, King Sudhodana, ruled over the Shakya people. Although the King hoped his son would carry on his legacy, the prince had a very different calling, one which made him one of history's most famous and influential figures.

In order to understand the principles of Buddhism, one must begin with the life of its founder. The deeds and words of Lord Buddha are the source and inspiration behind this popular faith. As you read the story of Buddha's enlightenment, note the place names on the map on page 11.

A Prince is Born

Prince Siddhartha, son of King Sudhodana and Queen Maya, was born around 563 BCE. Even before the birth, the queen had premonitions of great happenings. Legend tells that in her dreams a radiant white elephant descended from the sky. As the elephant descended, its six large tusks pierced the queen's womb, and she was filled with light.

That morning, the king and queen sought the counsel of the wise, for this was no ordinary dream. The fortune tellers explained that the queen would give birth to a son, and he would be a great leader. The couple was overjoyed at hearing this. King Sudhodana was thrilled, for now he would have a successor.

About ten months later, on the full moon night, in the Indian month of *Vaisakha* (May/June), Queen Maya was on her way to her father's house in the town of Lumbini.

A Prince is Born *(cont.)*

Suddenly, she halted her escorts, descended from her carriage, and entered a lush, beautiful garden. There she gave birth to a son. Legends tell of the sacred silence which anointed the garden that night and of a peace which flowed throughout the land.

The royal couple decided to name the baby Siddhartha, which means "the one who brings all good." News of the prince's birth spread, and there was much celebration. Many visitors came to pay tribute to Siddhartha. One of these visitors was the holy sage, Asita. Asita told the parents that the prince would be either a great king or a great saint. Then something strange happened. When Asita's eyes met the infant's, the sage began to weep. This worried the king and queen, but Asita explained that these were bittersweet tears he shed for himself, for he saw that this indeed was a special child, one who could lead others to peace. Now the holy man wept because, after a lifetime of searching, he would not live to hear Siddhartha's teachings.

Both the king and queen were happy, but Sudhodana wanted to be certain that his son became a great emperor, not a saint. Therefore, he set out to give Siddhartha all he could desire.

But the couple's joy was quickly ended when Queen Maya shortly became seriously ill. Within seven days of giving birth, she lay on her bed dying. She asked her sister, Prajapati, to mother her son. Prajapati consented. Soon afterwards, the queen passed away.

Young Prince Siddhartha

Prajapati raised Siddhartha as though he were her own son, and the prince lived a carefree childhood within the palace walls. King Sudhodana made certain that the boy received the finest education, for Asita's prophecy remained with him. The prince learned quickly. In fact, legend has it that after only a few lessons he had no need of teachers—he had learned all they could teach him.

Young Prince Siddhartha *(cont.)*

As Siddhartha grew, his intelligence was matched with a compassionate gentleness. Unlike his peers, he spent a great deal of time alone, wandering the palace gardens. He did not participate in the common games of boys but sought the company of animals and nature.

It was on one of these garden days that the prince came upon a wounded white swan, an arrow still piercing its wing. He removed the arrow and comforted the bird, tending to its wounds. Shortly thereafter, Devadatta, Siddhartha's cousin, came running. Adorned with bow and arrow, Devadatta demanded the swan he had hunted. But the prince refused. The boys argued until they agreed to settle their dispute in the palace's court.

When Devadatta came before the judges, he claimed that because he shot the bird, it should belong to him. When Siddhartha spoke, he said that he had saved the swan's life, and therefore it belonged to him. The judges sided with the prince, agreeing that the bird's savior has a greater right.

Siddhartha the Suitor

Years went by, and as the prince became a young man he continued in his gentle, quiet ways. This disturbed his father, who wanted his son more involved in worldly matters. But the king's worries were allayed when Siddhartha met Princess Yasodhara, daughter of King Suprabuddha. The young couple wanted to be married, but the neighboring king needed proof of Siddhartha's bravery and skills. Only then would he give his daughter in marriage. Although he had little experience in warrior games, the prince gladly agreed to take part in a contest against other suitors. Now even Siddhartha's father was worried. How could the prince compete against the other young men who had spent years in training?

Siddhartha the Suitor *(cont.)*

But the prince surprised everyone with his abilities. He began by winning the archery match, defeating his cousin, Devadatta. Next, he won the swordsmanship contest when, in one lightning quick stroke, he slashed through a tree—a tree with two trunks! However, though the prince was powerful, it was his gentleness which won him the final contest.

Each of the suitors was given an opportunity to mount a wild horse. One by one they were thrown by the wild, kicking beast. In fact, the horse was so ferocious that the judges were about to stop. But when Siddhartha approached the horse, stroking it softly and speaking kind words, the horse mellowed. The prince mounted the horse, and the contest was over. Prince Siddhartha and Princess Yasodhara were wed.

Although King Sudhodana was happy, he remained worried that his son may yet become a saint. So, he built the newlyweds three enormous, heavenly palaces—one for winter, one for summer, and the other for fall. These dwellings were surrounded by walls. Only beautiful servants, accomplished musicians, and the finest foods were allowed in the lush, natural settings. In this way, the king hoped Siddhartha would never be disturbed or seek to go outside the palace, and for years the prince and princess lived undisturbed within the palace walls. In time, they gave birth to a son, Rahula.

Outside the Palace Walls

Now, although Siddhartha had all the luxuries in the world, he had yet to do one thing: venture outside the palace grounds. From servants he heard tales of other lands and wonders of different peoples, languages, and landscapes. A stirring began inside him. Shortly after, he asked his father's permission to visit the capital city of his kingdom. The king consented, but he ordered his subjects to hide away anyone who was ill or old and to decorate their houses in festive colors, for Sudhodana did not want any sights to trouble his son.

The Story of Buddha

Outside the Palace Walls (cont.)

So, aboard his chariot the prince entered the city of Kapilavastu. The streets, lined with onlookers, were filled with gaiety and celebration. The cheerful citizens, all of them healthy and young, showered the prince with praise. For a moment, Siddhartha was pleased, thinking that this city was like his beloved palace, but it was then he saw an elderly man in the crowd, saddened and bent with age. In all his years, the prince had never seen such a sight. In fact, he did not even know that people grew old. This knowledge stunned him, and when he returned to the palace, he sat alone in deep contemplation.

In time, the prince journeyed again into the city, and again the streets were lined with happy faces. However, among the citizens was a sick man, coughing and pale. In all his palace years, sickness was unknown to Siddhartha. Now, he learned of disease. He learned that anyone can fall ill at anytime. This news saddened him.

But the prince's third trip to the city affected him most deeply. Riding along in his chariot, he saw a group of mourners carrying a coffin. Inside the coffin, he saw a dead man wrapped in white. Now he learned of death and the rites of cremation. He was overwhelmed with the thought that even his beloved wife and son would someday die.

Siddhartha became very depressed and spent his time alone. His father tried to cheer him, but to no avail. The prince wondered how people could live happily knowing that old age, sickness, and death awaited them. His gloom deepened, until one day he rode out again on his chariot. This time, he traveled to the countryside. There he saw a saint meditating under a tree. He learned that this hermit had exchanged all worldly pleasures to seek for truth. This man had also seen the suffering in the world and sought to go beyond it to enlightenment. Prince Siddhartha was deeply moved by the sight. He returned to the palace, sure of his calling.

Outside the Palace Walls *(cont.)*

Siddhartha's mind was made up: he would leave his life of luxury and search for truth. Knowing he would not receive consent, that very night as everyone lay sleeping, he bid a silent farewell to his wife and son. He mounted his horse and set out for the forest in the far reaches of the land where the holy men gather. When he arrived, he cut his long hair and donned the robe of an ascetic, a man of solitude searching for wisdom. Now, at the age of twenty-nine, his journey had begun.

The Search for Truth

Prince Siddhartha spent the next six years in the forest. He studied with the most famous sages, but still he did not find an end to suffering. He joined a group of men who believed enlightenment could be found by denying the body nourishment and sleep, thereby mastering pain. For years the prince ate and slept very little. He grew as thin as a skeleton, and though the rain and sun beat down on him, he did not waver from his practices.

Finally, he realized that he was getting nowhere. Though he had neglected his bodily needs, he had not found an end to suffering. Thus, when a young woman came to him offering food, he accepted. Now that he was nourished he sat in meditation under a bodhi tree in the town of Bodh-gaya. He sat down and vowed, come what may, he would not move until he found an end to sorrow. Although demons tempted him with images of his past and evil spirits brought nightmares upon him, the prince was centered on his goal.

Finally, under the Tree of Enlightenment, Siddhartha became Buddha, the Enlightened One. He went on to become a great world teacher, as Asita had prophesied, and from his teachings, Buddhism was born.

Places in the Life of Buddha

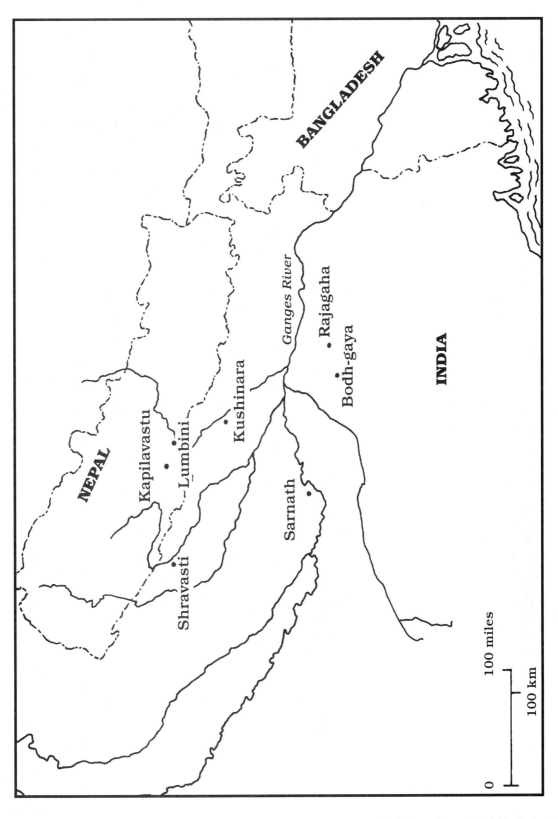

NEPAL

BANGLADESH

Kapilavastu

Lumbini

Kushinara

Shravasti

Sarnath

Ganges River

Rajagaha

Bodh-gaya

INDIA

100 miles

100 km

The Story of Buddha

Comprehension Questions

Directions: Use the information from pages 5–11 to answer the following questions.

1. When was Prince Siddhartha born? What does his name mean?

   _____

2. Describe Queen Maya's dream. What does it mean?

   _____

3. Why does the sage Asita weep when he sees Siddhartha?

   _____

4. What is Asita's prophesy about the prince?

   _____

5. What becomes of Queen Maya?

   _____

6. What does the king do to ensure Siddhartha's fulfillment?

   _____

7. As a child, how does the prince spend most of his time?

   _____

8. What happens when the prince finds a wounded swan?

   _____

9. Why must Siddhartha enter a contest to win Princess Yasodhara's hand in marriage?

   _____

10. The prince triumphs in three contests. Name them.

    _____

11. What does King Sudhodana give the prince and princess? Why?

    _____

12. List the three troubling sights Siddhartha witnesses during the visits to Kapilavastu.

    _____

13. What symbolic act does the prince perform when he arrives at the forest? How old is he when he arrives?

    _____

14. Why does Siddhartha starve himself and sleep very little?

    _____

15. In what city and under what kind of tree does Siddhartha become enlightened?

    _____

    _____

Critical Thinking

Directions: Answer the following questions, using details to support your responses.

1. Why do the palace judges award the wounded swan to Siddhartha? Do you agree with their decision? Explain.

   _____

   _____

   _____

2. Discuss King Sudhodana'a actions throughout the story. What are his motivations for sheltering Siddhartha?

   _____

   _____

   _____

3. Describe Siddhartha's feelings when he sees old age, sickness, and death. How does his upbringing contribute to his reaction?

   _____

   _____

   _____

4. In his search for enlightenment, Prince Siddhartha leaves behind his wife and son. In so doing, he became one of the most influential figures in history. Do you feel he is justified in leaving his family behind? Explain.

   _____

   _____

   _____

5. Can you think of someone other than Siddhartha who left behind a life of luxury in order to pursue wisdom? Explain.

   _____

   _____

   _____

Buddha's Teachings

The Buddhist Belief

After his enlightenment under the bodhi tree at Bodh-gaya, Buddha (the "Awakened One") began teaching others. Once he truly understood the cause of sorrow, he could begin to free people. What, then, did he teach?

Buddha delivered his first sermon in a deer park in the city of Sarnath. His first serman was called the Turning of the Wheel of Dharma—which represented his mission. He taught that all humans go through lifetimes in a cycle of birth and death, creating situations which create consequences. Until an individual can free him or herself from the wheel, he or she will be subject to the ups and downs of life. The only way to free oneself, preached Buddha, is to be free of desire. Thus, desire is the root of suffering. Then he taught his first disciples *The Four Noble Truths*. These truths form the bedrock of the Buddhist belief.

The Four Noble Truths

I. **Dukkha: The Noble Truth of Suffering**

Life is full of suffering, full of sickness and unhappiness. Although there are passing pleasures, they vanish in time.

II. **Samudaya: The Noble Truth of the Cause of Suffering**

People suffer for one simple reason: they desire things. It is greed and self-centeredness which bring about suffering. Desire is never satisfied.

III. **Nirodha: The Noble Truth of the End of Suffering**

It is possible to end suffering if one is aware of his or her own desires and puts an end to them. This awareness will open the door to lasting peace (*Nibbāna* or *Nirvana*).

IV. **Magga: The Noble Truth of the Path**

By changing one's thinking and behavior, a new awakening can be reached. This is called the *Middle Way* which constitutes the *Noble Eightfold Path*.

Buddha's Teachings

Buddhist Law

The *Noble Eightfold Path*, also called the *Wheel of Law*, contains eight steps for eliminating *dukkha* (suffering). By following this path, one can bring an end to his or her own *karma* and be released from continuous rebirth. Buddha introduced these ideas during his first sermon at Sarnath. This teaching is often symbolized by a wheel with eight spokes.

The Noble Eightfold Path

- **Right Understanding**

  Strive to clearly understand the Four Noble Truths. Strive to understand the workings of your own mind.

- **Right Thought**

  Think kindly of others and avoid dwelling on the past or future.

- **Right Speech**

  Speak kindly and truthfully. Do not use foul language or vain talk.

- **Right Action**

  Act kindly toward all living things. Do not be attached to the results of actions. Avoid killing, stealing, and intoxication.

- **Right Work**

  Have a vocation that does not harm others.

- **Right Effort**

  Be determined to cleanse the mind.

- **Right Mindfulness**

  Be fully aware of what you are doing, always with concern for others.

- **Right Concentration**

  Intensely concentrate during meditation to focus on being one with any situation.

The *Five Precepts* represent the third set of laws governing Buddhist thought. Although these are not "commandments" in the strict sense of the word, they are vows which ensure right behavior.

The Five Precepts

- **Do not harm any living thing.**
- **Do not steal. Take only what is given.**
- **Avoid over-stimulation.**
- **Do not say unkind things; avoid falsehoods.**
- **Do not take alcohol or drugs.**

The Wheel of Law

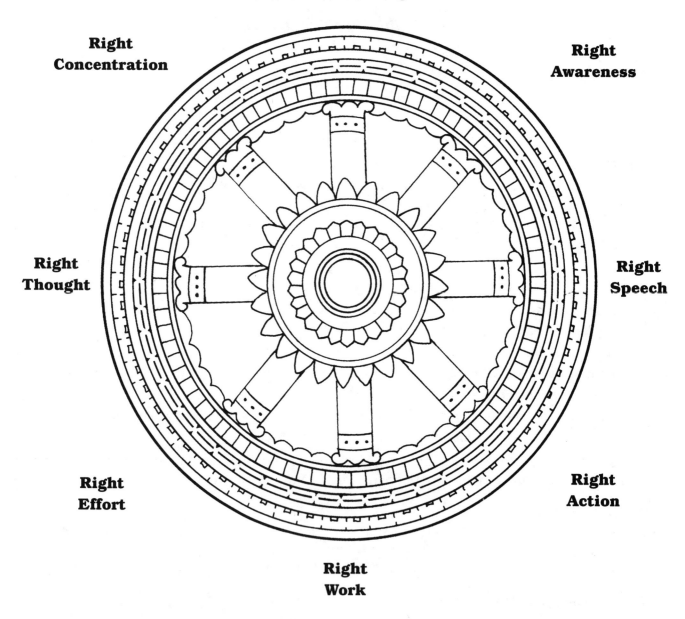

Right
Understanding

Right
Concentration

Right
Awareness

Right
Thought

Right
Speech

Right
Effort

Right
Action

Right
Work

The Eightfold Path

Directions: There are millions of Buddhists around the world trying to live in the spirit of the *Noble Eightfold Path*. Opportunities to live in the spirit of the path appear in many different ways. For each idea, write an example of how a person might show this step.

1. Right Understanding

   _____

   _____

2. Right Thought

   _____

   _____

3. Right Speech

   _____

   _____

4. Right Action

   _____

   _____

5. Right Work

   _____

   _____

6. Right Effort

   _____

   _____

7. Right Mindfulness

   _____

   _____

8. Right Concentration

   _____

   _____

The Main Branches

There are two main branches of Buddhism, **Theravada** and **Mahayana**. These schools of thought formed after Buddha's death in 486 BCE when disciples began disputing one another's interpretations of the Master's sayings.

Theravada Buddhism

The Theravada branch, also called the "doctrine of the elders," is most popular in Southern Asia in countries like Burma, Thailand, Laos, Sri Lanka, and Cambodia. (See the map on page 20.) The basis of the faith is that an individual is responsible for his or her own salvation. No god or image can bring enlightenment. Only by following the example of Buddha's life can an individual be free from the chain of rebirths. To a Theravada Buddhist, a person must be responsible for every act and thought. Salvation is by an individual's effort and not by grace of a supernatural power or being. At the earliest phase of Buddhism, the goal of salvation was achieved by being a disciple and attaining the state of Arahet (worthy one). Although there are no priests, these monks teach other Buddhists. They live in monasteries where they study the words and deeds of Buddha, striving to live pure lives and thereby achieve *nirvana*, enlightenment.

Mahayana Buddhism

Mahayana Buddhism is most common in countries of Northern Asia: Tibet, Nepal, China, Korea, and Japan. This school differs in some fundamental ways from the Theravadas. First of all, Mahayana Buddhists believe that religious growth is achieved through buddhahood and helping others to teach enlightenment. This tradition is called the "great vehicle." Spiritual growth can be nurtured through the help of others, especially those who have vowed to save others, namely Bodhisattvas. They maintain reverence and seek help from a bodhisattva (*bodhi* means "wise" and *sattva* means "being"). A bodhisattva is a saint who is so full of compassion that he will not enter into a state of nirvana until others can enter with him. You will learn more about some of these bodhisattvas later.

Mahayana Buddhism as it proceeded to adopt grace, devotion, and ritual has attracted more followers than Southern Buddhism. Monastics, temples, and gods have been established as the faith spread worldwide. Again, the most fundamental doctrine here is that people are not isolated but part of a network of all sentient beings. Some of these beings are more evolved, thereby able to guide others. Finally, it is believed that the spirit of Buddha is universal and timeless. It was discovered by Prince Siddhartha, but it is accessible to all. In fact, Mahayanas believe there have been others who have embodied that same spirit. Buddhists of all traditions await the coming of Maitreya, the Buddha of the coming age.

Two other branches stem from the Mahayanas: Tibetan Buddhism and Zen Buddhism. You will learn more about these branches later on.

Mahayana and Theravada Buddhism in Asia

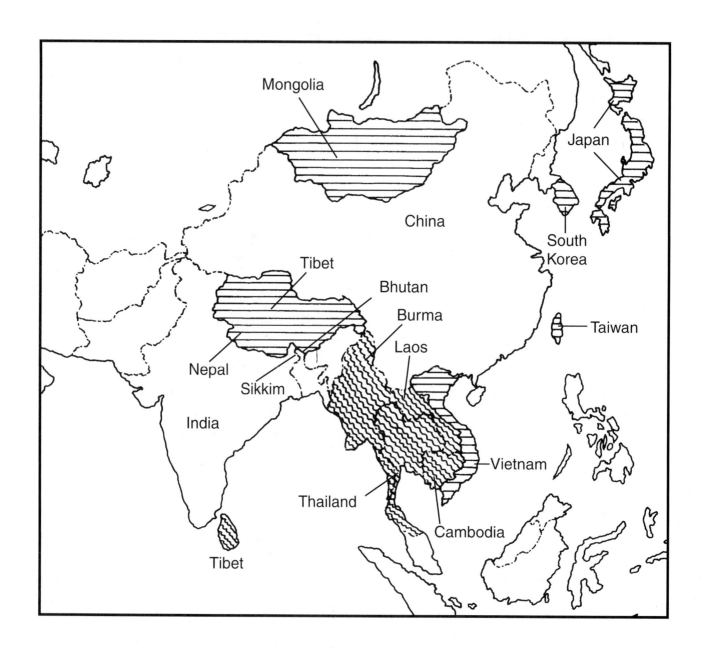

Mongolia

Japan

China

South
Korea

Tibet

Bhutan

Burma

Laos

Taiwan

Nepal

Sikkim

Vietnam

India

Thailand

Cambodia

Tibet

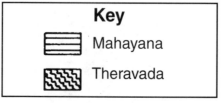

Key	
	Mahayana
	Theravada

Branches of Buddhism

Comprehension Questions

Directions: After reading pages 18 and 19, answer the following questions.

1. Describe the basic beliefs of Theravada (or Southern) Buddhism.

   _____

   _____

   _____

2. Describe the basic ideas of Mahayana Buddhism.

   _____

   _____

   _____

   _____

   _____

   _____

   _____

3. What is a *Bodhisattva?*

   _____

   _____

   _____

4. What two schools of Buddhism come from Mahayana Buddhism?

   _____

   _____

Buddhism in Asia

Buddhism began to spread rapidly around 270 BCE during the reign of King Asoka, the ruler of the greater area of Northern India. After engaging in a terrible, bloody war of succession against his half brother, he underwent a spiritual transformation that included embracing Buddhism. He sent missionaries throughout southern Asia and as far as Egypt, Syria, and Macedonia. They met with great success, although they did not convert others through either excessive persuasion or violence.

Beginning in the first century CE, Buddhism spread slowly into central Asia, China, Korea, and Japan. The first Dalai Lama, the Grand Lama of Lhasa, was responsible for spreading Buddhism into Mongolia during the 16th century CE.

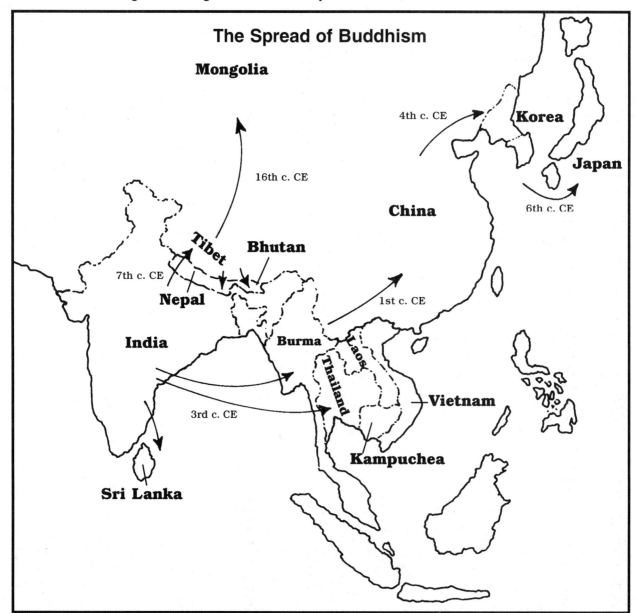

Holy Scriptures

From the two main branches of Buddhism— Theravada and Mahayana—come different sets of holy scriptures. Both texts come about after Buddha's death, though they were not translated into written form for close to 500 years. Instead, they were passed on by word of mouth.

The Theravada scriptures were reduced to writing in 80 BCE by Sri Lankans who wrote in the Indian language of *Pali*. They called these teachings the *Tipitaka*, which are divided into three "baskets of law." The first basket, the *Vinaya Pitaka*, contains the laws governing the life of a Buddhist monk or nun. The second basket, the *Sutta Pitaka*, contains dialogues and teachings delivered by Buddha himself. The third basket, the *Abhidamma Pitaka*, contains commentary on Buddha's teachings. The fundamental doctrine of all traditions of Buddhism are based on these early scriptures.

Sanskrit, the ancient language of India, was the means for transmitting the Mahayana scriptures. Although many of the earlier Mahayana scriptures were destroyed, their messages were kept alive in the writings of Tibetan and Chinese sages. There are now several of these scriptures recognized by Mahayana Buddhists. One of these sacred texts is a long poem written around 690 CE by Seng Ts'an, a Chinese sage. The poem is called "Trust in the Heart."

Trust in the Heart

The Perfect Way is only difficult for those who pick and choose;
Do not like, do not dislike; all will then be clear.
Make a hairbreadth difference, and Heaven and Earth are set apart.
If you want the truth to stand clear before you, never be for or against.
The struggle between "for" and "against" is the mind's worst disease;
While the deep meaning is misunderstood, it is useless to meditate on them.
It is as blank and featureless as space; it has no "too little" or "too much";
Only because we take and reject does it mean to us not to be so.
Do not chase after Enlightenment as though it were a real thing;
Do not try to drive pain away by pretending that it is not real;
Pain, if you seek serenity in Oneness, will vanish of its own accord.
Stop all movement in order to get rest, and rest will itself be restless;
Linger over either extreme and Oneness is forever lost.
Those who cannot attain Oneness in either case will fail.
To banish reality is to sink deeper into the Real . . .

Buddhist Scriptures

Holy Scriptures *(cont.)*

The Sutta Pitaka records actual dialogues and sermons of Buddha himself. On page 25 is an excerpt from one of these teachings. Read the excerpt in a group or as a class, and discuss what you think is being taught in the passage. What do you think Buddha means when he talks about Mara? Discuss why knowledge is a weapon.

Use the space below and a dictionary to write the meanings of some of the words you do not know from the passage.

_____

_____

_____

_____

_____

_____

_____

_____

_____

_____

_____

_____

_____

_____

_____

_____

Holy Scriptures *(cont.)*

Thought

As an arrow-maker makes straight his arrow, a wise man makes straight his trembling and unsteady thought, which is difficult to guard, difficult to hold back.

As a fish taken from his watery home and thrown on the dry ground, our thought trembles all over in order to escape the dominion of Mara, the tempter.

It is good to tame the mind, which is difficult to hold in and flighty, rushing wherever it lists; a tamed mind brings happiness.

Let the wise man guard his thoughts, for they are difficult to perceive, very subtle, and they rush wherever they list; thoughts well-guarded bring happiness.

Those who bridle their mind, which travels far, moves about alone, is incorporeal, and hides in the chamber of the heart, will be free from the bonds of Mara, the tempter.

If a man's faith is unsteady, if he does not know the true law, if his peace of mind is troubled, his knowledge will never be perfect.

If a man's thoughts are not scattered, if his mind is not perplexed, if he has ceased to think of good or evil, then there is no fear for him while he is watchful.

Knowing that his body is fragile like a jar, and making his thought firm like a fortress, one should attack Mara, the tempter, with the weapon of knowledge; one should watch him when conquered, and should never rest.

Tibetan Buddhism

Background Information for the Teacher

Presented below are historical highlights of the origins of Tibetan Buddhism. Share the information with students. Discuss some basic beliefs of Tibetan Buddhism and the importance of the Dalai Lama. Then, read and discuss the bodhisattvas (gods) on page 27. Encourage students to find out more about each bodhisattva.

The map on page 22 represents Buddhist expansion into Tibet in the 7th century CE, more than 1,500 years ago. The people of Tibet are mostly nomadic, moving about the high Himalayan plateaus with their herds. For centuries, Mahayana Buddhism thrived in this rugged, undeveloped country.

Until China invaded Tibet in 1950, this vast natural setting was spotted with Buddhist monasteries. In fact, Buddhism defines both the religious and political climate of Tibet. The ruler of the country, the Dalai Lama, is chosen on a belief that he will be reborn to resume his place in a series of rebirths. His compassion and wisdom are meant to inspire the people. Like the Catholic Pope, the Tibetan Dalai Lama is believed to be the closest link to the spiritual realm.

The most important quality of the Dalai Lama is compassion. In fact, Tibetan Buddhists believe that the Dalai Lama is a manifestation of the bodhisattva Avalokiteshvara. This god embodies the spirit of compassion, the same spirit alive in Buddha. The Dalai Lama is, therefore, a vehicle in which the bodhisattva's mercy can radiate to the people. Finding the Dalai Lama, however, is not always easy.

Tibetans believe that when the Dalai Lama dies, Avalokiteshvara is reborn as a baby. The Dalai Lama usually gives some indication of the baby's whereabouts, after which the search begins. Lamas, Tibetan monks, quest for the newborn, looking for proof of his heritage. They put the candidate through different tests.

A true Dalai Lama, for instance, should recognize four of the previous ruler's possessions.

Besides the Dalai Lama, there exist up to 200 tulkus. These holy men and women are also revered as embodiments of Avalokiteshvara. These leaders are often responsible for spreading the message of Buddhism.

In 1950, Tibet was conquered by communist China. The Chinese government held that Tibet was part of their country. Although the Tibetans rebelled, the Chinese took over, destroying most of the monasteries and causing most of the monks and nuns to flee the country. Many Tibetans settled in India, while others exiled themselves to the West.

Avalokiteshvara

Avalokiteshvara is one of the foremost bodhisattvas. Tibetan Buddhists consider this saint to be the spirit of Buddha. They also believe the Dalai Lama is a reincarnation of Avalokiteshvara.

Tara

In Tibet, the goddess Tara is the consort of Avalokiteshvara. She is an embodiment of compassion.

Manjushri

Manjushri, the destroyer of ignorance, wields the Sword of Knowledge.

Amida

To northern Buddhists, Amida is next to Buddha himself in importance. Legend has it that Amida was a monk who devoted himself to saving others. Over the centuries, he has stored up a treasury of goodness which the faithful can access, thus freeing them from the Wheel of Life. He presides over western paradise, a heaven to which believers go if they recite his name at the time of death.

Extensions

1. Find an illustration of the bodhisattva Maitreya, the Buddha to come.
2. Find colored illustrations of the bodhisattvas and color the saints here, accordingly.

Zen Buddhism

Background Information for the Teacher

Presented below are highlights of the origins and beliefs of Zen Buddhism. Share the information with students. Discuss some of the basic beliefs of Zen Buddhism with the class. Have students read about haiku poetry on page 29 and encourage them to write their own haiku poems.

The Spirit of Zen

Transmission outside doctrine,
No dependencies on words.
Pointing directly at the mind,
Thus seeing oneself truly,
Attaining Buddhahood.

–Bodhidharma, 520 CE

This poem, written by the famous Indian monk, Bodhidharma, embodies the spirit of Zen Buddhism, a school of thought born in China around 520 CE. Zen arrived in China in 1191. Zen is the Japanese transformation of the Korean word *Son* which is derived from the Chinese *Ch'an*. Unlike other branches of Buddhism, Zen places no emphasis on either scriptures or bodhisattvas. Rather, practitioners of Zen believe that direct experience alone can lead one to truth. In other words, scriptures and teachers can serve only to point to enlightenment. It is the individual who must live and understand. In fact, mentors and theories must be destroyed before the mind is free, because their ideas and opinions about enlightenment prevent understanding. This point is illustrated in a story of a well known Zen master who shocked his students by tossing all the statues of Buddha into a fire in order to warm the room. Like these clay idols, images should be burned out of the mind: a person must be self-reliant, his or her own master.

Students of Zen practice meditation in order to increase their awareness and purify their minds. They hope to undo their opinions and preferences and reach a state of *satori*, or illumination. With this clarity, they can live calmly and compassionately in the world. A poem by the Chinese master, Tessho, describes this freedom of mind:

Finally out of reach—
No bondage, no dependency.
How calm the ocean,
Towering the void.

Although Zen does not emphasize scripture, it has a rich body of literature which points to understanding. Besides poetry, these books contain dialogues between pupils and teachers. These discussions are meant to bring understanding to the reader.

Zen Buddhism also finds expression in the martial arts, which arrived in Japan about 800 years ago. The schools of karate and judo, among others, are meant to enhance discipline and self-awareness. Gardening is also a popular expression of the Zen spirit. These gardens are simple but exact, mirroring the tranquility of Zen.

Japanese Poetry

You may already be familiar with the most popular form of Zen poetry, *haiku*. Haiku began in Japan during the 15th century CE. It began as a 17-syllable stanza but soon became a poem by itself. (The poems below are translations, so the syllable count is not exact.) Still popular among poets, haiku is concise, combining images to produce emotion and meaning. Most often, haiku is a celebration of nature and the wholeness and union of all living things.

Here are several haikus written by famous Japanese poets. Read them carefully and pay attention to the imagery. How does each one make you feel? After reading, write some of your own. Each three-line poem must have five syllables in the first and third lines and seven in the second.

To the willow—
all hatred, and desire
of your heart.
　　　—Basho

White lotus—
the monk
draws back his blade.
　　　—Buson

Under cherry trees
there are
no strangers.
　　　—Issa

Dew of the bramble,
thorns
sharp white.
　　　—Buson

Sacred night,
through masks
white breath of dancers.
　　　—Kikaku

Come, see
real flowers
of this painful world.
　　　—Basho

Buddha's Nirvana,
beyond flowers,
and money.
　　　—Issa

May he who brings
flowers tonight,
have moonlight.
　　　—Kikaku

Here is a 17-syllable haiku:
The light rising fast (5)
Over the far eastern plains (7)
Brings daytime to all. (5)

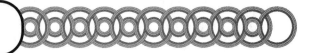

How to Meditate

You have probably heard the word "meditation" many times in your life. You may have seen pictures of people sitting in meditation with crossed legs and eyes closed. You may even know someone who meditates. But what exactly is meditation? What is its purpose?

In all traditions of Buddhism, followers meditate in order to still their minds, to let go of the running thoughts inside their brains and purify it of greed, hatred, and ignorance. If you stop to notice, thoughts go on from the moment of waking until sleep. They even appear in dreams. For Buddhists, meditation is a means of finding what lies beyond these thoughts. Of course, this takes practice.

There are many forms of meditation. Usually, Buddhists sit still, spine straight and eyes closed. By focusing on their breath, they become more "present," more aware of themselves. Although the stream of thoughts continues, the student simply watches them go by like clouds in the sky. Thus, he or she begins to be free of the grip of thinking.

Zen Buddhists have some unusual entries to meditation practices. One such entry is called a koan, or a riddle. The master asks a puzzling question which the student must answer correctly—although it may take days to comprehend! Thus, the koan provides the means for meditation.

Tibetan Buddhists like to focus on *mandalas* during meditation. Mandalas are elaborate designs rich with color and detail. They are often circular, containing either portraits of various gods or intricate patterns. After meditating on the mandala, the student will close his or her eyes and try to visualize the picture. Thus, the mind is disciplined while the heart merges with the spirit of the mandala.

Extension

Try sitting quietly five minutes a day. Just sit and listen to the sounds around you, even the sound of your breathing. After a few days, try ten minutes. Keep a journal of your "quiet time" experiences.

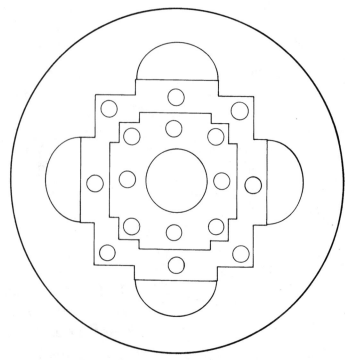

Mandalas

Directions: Below you will find three different mandalas. Color them. Then, try designing one of your own!

Typical Design

Tibetan

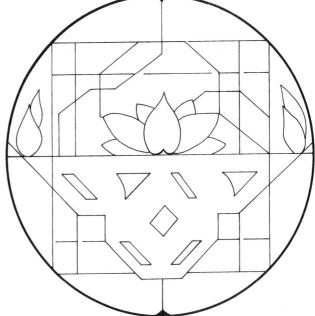

Sri Yantra

My Own Design

Rites of Passage

Unlike most other faiths, Buddhism does not require strict observance of custom. Because Buddhism is so focused on the internal life, some Buddhists practice privately without visiting temples or participating in rituals. Most, however, visit temples regularly, seek the counsel of monks, and partake in rites of passage ceremonies. These ceremonies differ greatly depending upon the country of origin.

Birth

When an infant is born, Theravadin Buddhists usually have the formal naming at a nearby temple. Afterward, monks bless and sprinkle holy water on the newborn. The closing ritual, the melting of candle wax into a bowl, symbolizes the union of the four basic elements: earth, air, fire, and water.

Marriage

In some Buddhist countries, monks never attend weddings because marriage ceremonies are a part of secular life. In most countries, however, Buddhist monks do attend. Take, for instance, the example of a common Theravadin wedding. The ceremony takes place at the local temple. Here the bride and groom are surrounded by friends and relatives. First, the image of Buddha or a casket of relics is wrapped with a long cotton thread, and then the thread circulates to all those in the congregation. The thread symbolizes the union of all present. All the while, the chanting of the monks fills the temple. After the principal monk blesses the couple, two pieces of the thread are cut. A monk ties one around the groom's wrist, and then the groom ties the other piece around the wrist of his bride. All present receive a piece of thread.

Rites of Passage

Death

Buddhists do not believe in the reincarnation of individual identities. Rather, it is the person's *dharma*, the balance of good and evil that is present in consciousness, which is cast into a new life. It is common for monks to visit the home of the dying person, comforting him or her with religious chants. These verses remind the person that although the body decays, goodness and mercy are timeless. This chanting continues even after death, in order to ensure purification of the soul.

According to Tibetan Buddhism, immediately after the moment of death, an individual experiences a state of trance or spirit-like existence which lasts from seven to forty-nine days. The deceased is not aware of his or her death. These days are called the *First Bardo*, during which monks can communicate with the dead by chanting certain verses. After these days, the person sees a very bright light. If the soul can embrace the light, it will be free of rebirth. Usually, however, the light's radiance frightens the deceased, in which case rebirth follows. The *Second Bardo* begins when a person sees the events and thoughts of his or her life. Now the knowledge of death is clear, and the *Third Bardo* starts. Now the deceased is free to choose new parents and a new identity.

Directions: There are many rituals, ceremonies, and even holidays dedicated to those who are born, marry, or die. Find out about your own family's traditions and beliefs concerning one of these stages of life. Do you have a ritual? How have things changed over time? Write your response below.

_____

_____

_____

_____

_____

_____

_____

_____

_____

_____

_____

Temples and Shrines

The Stupa

The design of Buddhist temples originated with the *stupa*, in which were enshrined Buddha's ashes and relics. Made out of mud bricks, this ancient Indian shrine is usually shaped like a simple bell—a mound with a small spire on top. Inside the stupas are Buddhist relics. The circular shape of the dome resembles the Wheel of Life.

Gradually, the stupa became larger and more elaborate. Soon, reliefs of Prince Siddhartha's life began appearing on its outer walls.

The world's largest stupa rests on the island of Java, Indonesia. Toward the top, this elegant Mahayana shrine contains grand images of Buddha and statues of bodhisattvas. Below, there are sculptures depicting the life of Buddha and the history of Buddhism. At the peak there is a large, plain stupa which represents enlightenment.

The Pagoda

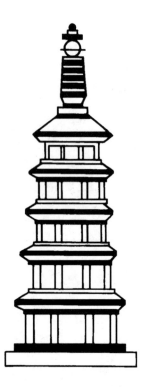

In China, the stupa grew taller and thinner and adopted a new identity: the *pagoda*. Pagodas are eight-sided towers which contain an odd number of stories—between three and seventeen. Soon pagodas of different architectural forms became popular; thousands were built throughout China, Japan, Vietnam, Thailand, and Burma. Although many of the older wooden pagodas have disappeared in east Asia, the architecture still lives on. In Japan, for example, small stone pagodas often appear in cemeteries. They have five levels, symbolizing the void and the four basic elements.

Temples and Shrines

The Monastery

The Buddhist monastery arose during the lifetime of Buddha. As early as 500 BCE, these structures provided shelter and study space for monks. Some monasteries, built for Buddha by kings and rich devotees, were sumptuous institutions. Some were made of stone or wood while others, amazingly, were forged out of mountains of rock later on. Monks literally carved their sanctuary into cliff sides in Western India and later on along the Silk Route in Central Asia and China. Once this was done, they designed the interior with an assembly hall and living quarters, including a small stupa at the heart of the monastery. Detailed reliefs of Buddha and various bohisattvas often decorate the rock walls.

Theravadin Shrine

Theravadin shrine rooms are relatively unadorned places of meditation. An elevated statue of Buddha, surrounded by offerings of incense, candles, and flowers, rest at the center. Tiles or carpet decorates the floor.

Temples and Shrines

• • • • • • • • • • • • • • • • • **Thai Temple** • • • • • • • • • • • • • • • • •

In Thailand, Buddhists temples, or *wats*, appear in almost every town. Attended to by monks, the wat is a place of worship and community gathering. Colorful and exotic, the temple contains three elements: a stupa, a bodhi tree, and a shrine room housing an image of Buddha.

Followers make offerings of flowers, incense, and fruit to the statue. Then, they may light a candle and chant stanza in Pali. The entrance to the temple, facing east, is decorated with curtains and serpent-like ornaments. The top of the wat is usually a towering pinnacle.

Wheel of Law

You are already familiar with the Dharma Wheel or the Wheel of Law. This sign is associated with Buddha's first sermon at a deer park in Sarnath. The wheel symbolizes the setting in motion of the Buddha's career as a missionary. The eight spokes of the wheel represent the eightfold path. Occasionally, in later versions, the hub contains images of the three causes of pain: the serpent of ill will, the pig of ignorance, and the rooster of lust.

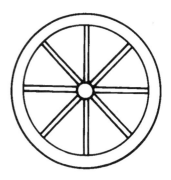

Lotus

Like many of the Hindu gods, the Buddha is often shown sitting on a lotus throne. In Buddhism, the lotus flower is meaningful because its roots are mired in the mud; yet its flowers bloom above water. This mirrors the life of Buddha who journeyed through a troubled world yet remained holy.

White Elephant

The White Elephant symbolizes the birth of Prince Siddhartha. The Prince's mother, Queen Maya, dreamt that a bright elephant of light descended upon her—a sign that her son would be great among men.

The Bodhi Tree

The bodhi tree in Bodh-gaya is sacred to Buddhists for it is here where Prince Siddhartha attained nirvana. The bodhi tree has become a symbol associated with Buddha's enlightenment. In Southern Buddhism, the second most important symbol of worship is the bodhi tree.

Rupas: Images of Buddha

These images, which are in several postures and gestures, are many, each with its own significance. Buddha is shown with a topknot of hair which signifies his superior wisdom. In each figure, his position is related to his actions—teaching, blessing, or meditating. As you will see, even his hand gestures, or mudras, have become traditional gestures. For the first 500 years of Buddhism, the Buddha was not represented, in human form. The image of Buddha, or rupas, is a creation of Kushans who imitated the Greek image of Apollo.

The Starving Prince Siddhartha

Lotus Pose

Japanese Buddha Dressed as Monk

Full Lotus Position for Meditation

Mantras and Mudras

Tibetan Buddhists use *mantras*, or chants, when they worship. These mantras consist of one or more sounds which, like the mandala and mudras (hand gestures), are meant to focus the mind and involve a state of grace. The most sacred sound, Om, has a Hindu origin. It is often part of a longer mantra which reads like this: Om Mani Padme Hum (pronounced "om manee padmey home"). Translated, it means "the jewel in the lotus" or "the heart of the teaching."

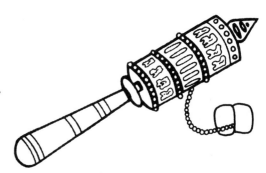

Among Tibetan Buddhisys, this prayer is often heard in the streets. It appears on flags above every temple and it is inscribed on prayer wheels. People spin these bronze cylinders either as hand-held prayer wheels or as prayer drums as a conventional form of worship.

Mudras are the hand positions of Buddha. They are used in Tibetan Buddhist worship as magical symbols. Each gesture has its own meaning. Try them yourself.

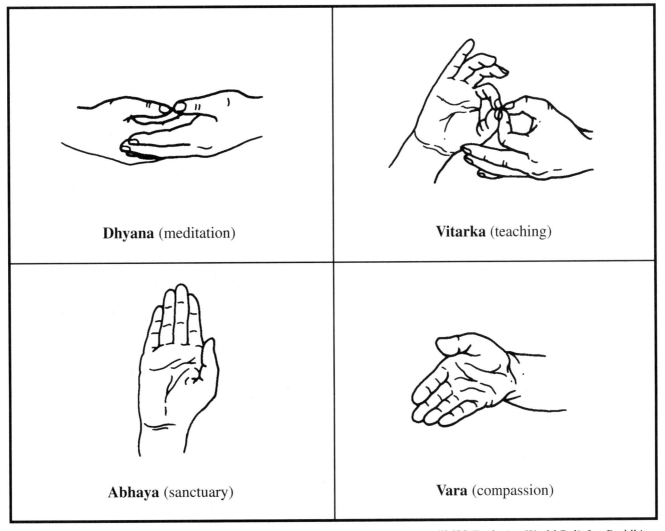

Dhyana (meditation)

Vitarka (teaching)

Abhaya (sanctuary)

Vara (compassion)

The Month of Vesak

According to Southern Buddhism, the month of Vesak (in May) contains holidays celebrating the birth, enlightenment, and death of Buddha. In some countries, all three events are celebrated on the full moon in May. Other schools of thought observe these events as individual holidays in different months of the year. Since 1950, Vesak has been observed by all Buddhist communities as the Buddha Day.

One of the common features of Vesak is the lantern. In Thailand, people also decorate their homes with garlands of flowers and attend temple ceremonies. Followers polish the temple's statues of Buddha. After dark, the images are sprinkled with scented water as the followers take up their lanterns and walk in a circle surrounding Buddha with light. This day of spiritual observances is also predominated by meditation.

Buddha's Birthday

In Japan, the birth of Buddha is celebrated on April 8 during a festival called *Hana Mastsuri*. Followers gather on the weekend nearest the holiday to ensure that they can attend. Outside the sanctuary, booths and games provide a festive atmosphere; however, at the heart of the shrine the mood is austere. The image of Buddha is strewn with flowers and surrounded with burning incense. People bow before the statue and pour a ladle of tea over it, thus commemorating the birth of Prince Siddhartha.

In the country of Laos, Buddha's birthday is combined with the New Year's celebration. During this lively festival, caged birds are set free and captured fish are returned to their native rivers. In temples and homes, holy water is poured on statues of Buddha. Then, the streets are busy with people drenching one another with buckets of water!

The Festival of the Tooth

The Festival of the Tooth takes place in the beautiful lakeside city of Kandy in Sri Lanka. On a hillock near the lake there is a temple which houses one of the most sacred Buddhist relics: Buddha's tooth. The tooth is kept hidden within seven jeweled caskets. But each year, on the full moon night in the month of Savana (August), a colorful procession transports a relic of Buddha through the city of Kandy. Pilgrims journey far distances to watch elephants, adorned with golden headdresses and silver jewels, parade the streets. Some of the elephants are caparisoned (covered, cloaked) with multicolored clothing on their mammoth backs. Aboard the largest elephant is a casket inside of which rests a relic of the Buddha. Followers celebrate as the relic passes by them, trailed by dancers and fire swallowers. The festival lasts two weeks.

Obon

Obon, or the Feast of Obon, is a popular Japanese holiday in which Buddhists pay homage to the dead. Tradition has it that on this day the souls of the deceased mix and mingle with the living. The making of paper boats is one of the many ceremonies of Obon. At daybreak, followers gather at a lake or stream and release the boats, transporting the souls of the dead.

The Feast of Obon is inspired by the legend of Maudgalyayana, a follower of Buddha. Maudgalyayana had a nightmare in which he saw his mother cast into the underworld. There, she joined other spirits who were tortured by having a banquet set before them, but when they tried to eat, the food turned to fire. The troubled man sought the counsel of Buddha, who advised him to practice kindness and to purify himself. The man became a generous monk, giving to all. After some years, he dreamed that his mother was free. Overjoyed, he set out a great feast for the villagers. In this spirit, Japanese Buddhists partake in a great feast.

The Buddhist Calendar

Like most religious calendars, the Buddhist calendar is based on the lunar year. That is, each month ends on a full moon, and most major festivals are celebrated on these days. Celebrations occur at different times depending on the country.

Here are the months of the Buddhist calendar along with their Gregorian equivalents. Below, you will also find a list of major festivals.

Citta (April)	Vesak (May)	Jettha (June)
Asalha (July)	Savana (August)	Potthapada (September)
Assayuja (October)	Kattika (November)	Maggasira (December)
Phussa (January)	Magha (February)	Phagguna (March)

Some Significant Festivals and Holidays

Citta: celebration of Buddha as peacemaker

Vesak: celebrations of the birth, enlightenment, and death of Buddha

Jettha: commemoration of the spread of Buddhism

Asalha: Buddha's journey from home and his first sermon

Savana: a special meditation retreat during the beginning of the rainy season when it is difficult for monks and nuns to travel

Kattika: end of the rainy season; Buddhist missionaries remembered

Maggasira: first community of Buddhist nuns founded in Sri Lanka

Phussa: celebration of Buddha's first visit to Sri Lanka

Phagguna: celebration of Buddha's return home

Places of Pilgrimage

India

The four primary places of Buddhist pilgrimage are located in India, Buddha's homeland. Pilgrims from all over the globe visit these holy places. Probably the most popular destination is the deer park in Sarnath where Buddha preached his first sermon. Sarnath is now a suburb of the sacred city of Varanasi. This location also features a gigantic stupa built by King Ashoka in honor of Lord Buddha.

King Ashoka also built a monument at Lumbini Grove in Nepal, where Prince Siddhartha was born and marked the spot with an inscribed stone pillar. Pilgrims who travel here will see an inscribed stone pillar which was built in honor of the holy birth.

At Bodh-gaya, followers behold the place of Buddha's enlightenment. In fact, an actual descendent of the ancient bodhi tree still exists. Under this tree, which is often decorated with prayer flags, rests a stone inscribed with a footprint. There are many who believe this is literally Buddha's own print.

Another place of pilgrimage is in Kusinara where Buddha died. People gather here to pay tribute and to visit the famous stupa containing the relics and ashes of Buddha.

Sri Lanka

Towering high in the central part of the island, Adam's Peak is the principal place of pilgrimage in Sri Lanka. Pilgrims ascend countless flights of steps in order to reach the summit where there rests a rock bearing the footprint of Buddha. Although it remains unclear whether or not Buddha ever went to Sri Lanka, some people believe that this print was left as a memento during his third visit to the island.

In addition, there are two famous monastery complexes in the two ancient capitals of Sri Lanka: Anaradhapura (400 BCE–1000CE) and Polunnaruwa (1100–1200CE). These contain massive and inspiring rock depictions of Buddha.

Tibet

One of the most popular religious sites in Tibet is Portala, the palace of the Dalai Lama, at the Lake of Padmasambhava. Padmasambhava is the founder of Tibetan Buddhism. Legend has it that from this lake he was born in a lotus blossom. This popular leader is said to have spread Buddha's teachings in exchange for bags of gold dust. When he had gathered a great amount of gold, he loosened the bags and the precious dust flew away in the breeze. In doing so, he wanted to prove that only what is eternal is of value.

Vocabulary Review

Directions: Match the letter of the appropriate definition to each vocabulary word.

_____ 1. stupa

_____ 2. bodhi tree

_____ 3. Vesak

_____ 4. Mahayana

_____ 5. King Ashoka

_____ 6. Siddhartha

_____ 7. haiku

_____ 8. Obon

_____ 9. mantra

_____ 10. monastery

_____ 11. Theravada

_____ 12. Queen Maya

_____ 13. bodhisattva

_____ 14. Dalai Lama

_____ 15. rupa

_____ 16. mandala

_____ 17. pagoda

_____ 18. King Sudhodana

_____ 19. mudras

_____ 20. Wheel of Law

A. principal Buddhist symbol

B. a compassionate deity

C. helped spread Buddhism

D. a design used for meditation

E. Southern branch of Buddhism

F. Siddhartha's father

G. mound-like building

H. where Buddha was enlightened

I. leader of Tibetan Buddhism

J. month of three celebrations

K. a position of the Buddha image

L. Northern branch of Buddhism

M. tall, thin tower

N. Siddhartha's mother

O. "one who brings all good"

P. short Japanese poem

Q. abodes for monks

R. a chant

S. conventionalized hand positions

T. Japanese holiday for the dead

Part One

For statements 1–10, fill in the spaces with the correct answers.

1. Prince Siddhartha was born around _____, in the garden of _____ .

2. The Four Noble Truths state that _____ is the root of suffering.

3. Three of the steps on the Eightfold path include right _____, right _____ and right _____ .

4. Three countries in which Theravada Buddhism is popular are _____ , _____ , and _____ .

5. Three countries in which Mahayana Buddhism is popular are _____ , _____ , and _____ .

6. The Theravadin scriptures are contained in the _____ .

7. Buddhists practice _____ in order to quiet their minds.

8. Some Zen Buddhists use riddles, or _____ , in their practice.

9. Buddhist architecture originated with the _____ .

10. The principle symbol of Buddhism is called _____ .

Part Two

Respond to the following prompts in the spaces below.

1. Why did King Sudhodana want his son to witness no suffering?

_____

_____

_____

2. List and explain briefly the Four Noble Truths.

_____

_____

_____

Part Two *(cont.)*

3. What is the purpose of meditation? What do Buddhists usually do when meditating?

_____

_____

_____

_____

_____

4. Explain the role of the Dalai Lama in Tibetan Buddhism. How is a new Dalai Lama chosen?

_____

_____

_____

5. Describe the features of a stupa, pagoda, and monastery.

_____

_____

_____

6. List and describe three places of pilgrimage for Buddhists.

_____

_____

_____

_____

7. What are some of the qualities most Buddhists strive to embody?

_____

_____

_____

_____

If you have ever read about something that happened long ago, then you are probably familiar with the abbreviations BC or BCE and AD or CE. Buddha was born in 563 BCE. Muhammad died in 632 CE. Both BC and BCE represent the years before the birth of Jesus. CE and AD mean the years after the birth of Jesus. The abbreviations stand for the following:

BC = Before Christ

AD = Anno Domini (in the year of our Lord)

BCE = Before the Common Era

CE = Common Era

In this book, only BCE and CE will be used.

You have probably also read of events happening, for example, in the 5th century or even in the 5th century BCE. A century is 100 years. If people lived in the 1st century, they lived in the first 100 years CE, or in the first 100 years after the birth of Jesus. So, if we say something happened in the 19th century, we mean it happened during the years 1801–1900 CE. The same rule applies to the centuries BCE, only we count backwards from the birth of Jesus. For example, Buddha was born in 563 BCE, which would mean he was born in the 6th century BCE.

Questions

Here are some practice questions. You will need to use the time line below and your math skills to find the answers.

2000 BCE	1500 BCE	1000 BCE	500 BCE	0	500 CE	1000 CE	1500 CE	2000 CE

1. Who is older, someone born in 1760 BCE or someone born in 1450 BCE?

   _____

2. How many years difference is there between 250 CE and 250 BCE?

   _____

3. How many years difference is there between 1524 CE and 1436 BCE?

   _____

4. You visit a cemetery. One of the tombstones reads: "Born in the 15th century, died in the 16th." Make up possible dates that this person may have been born and died.

   _____

5. In what century are you living now?

   _____

Answer Key

Page 12

1. He was born in 563 BCE. His name means "the one who brings all good."
2. A white elephant pierced her womb. She would give birth to a great leader.
3. Asita weeps because after a lifetime of searching, he would not live to hear Siddhartha's teachings.
4. He will be either a great ruler or a great teacher.
5. She dies shortly after giving birth.
6. The king showers him with pleasure and protects him from ugliness.
7. He spends most of his time communing with nature.
8. He rescues it.
9. King Suprabuddha needed proof of Siddhartha's bravery.
10. He triumphs in archery, swordsmanship, and horsemanship.
11. He gives them three palaces to protect them from the outside world.
12. He sees an old man, a sick man, and a dead man.
13. He cut his long hair; he was 29 years old.
14. He had joined a group of men who believed that enlightenment could be found by denying the body of nourishment and sleep.
15. Siddhartha became enlightened under the bodhi tree in the city of Bodh-gaya.

Page 13

Answers will vary.

Page 21

1. The underlying basis of Theravada Buddhism is that an individual is responsible for his or her own salvation. They follow the example of Buddha's life studying words and deeds of Buddha and living pure lives to achieve enlightenment.
2. In Mahayana Buddhism, religious growth can be nurtured through the help of others. Followers maintain reverence and seek help from a Bodhisattva. They believe that people are not isolated but part of a network of beings. They believe that the spirit of Buddha is universal and others have embodied the spirit of Buddha.
3. A Bodhisattva is a saint, a wise being from whom Mahayana Buddhists seek help from.
4. Tibetan Buddhism and Zen Buddhism are derived from Mahayana Buddhism.
5. Answers will vary.

Page 44

1. G	6. O	11. E	16. D
2. H	7. P	12. N	17. M
3. J	8. T	13. B	18. F
4. L	9. R	14. I	19. S
5. C	10. Q	15. K	20. A

Pages 45 and 46
Part One

1. 563 BCE, Lumbini
2. desire
3. Answers will vary.
4. Answers will vary.
5. Answers will vary.
6. Tipitaka
7. meditation
8. koans
9. stupa
10. The Dharma Wheel or the Wheel of Law

Part Two

1. The king was afraid Siddhartha would become a saint after seeing the realities of the world.
2. The Four Noble Truths are suffering, cause of suffering, end of suffering, and truth of the path.
3. The purpose of meditation is to still and purify the mind, to let go of the running thoughts inside the brain. Buddhists usually sit still, spine straight, and eyes closed as they focus on breathing. Zen buddhists use a koan. Tibetan buddhists focus on mandalas.
4. The Dalai Lama is the spiritual and political leader of Tibet; a baby is sought with information given by Dalai Lama, then the baby is tested for special knowledge.
5. See page 34 descriptions and diagrams of temples and shrines.
6. Three places of pilgrimage include the deer park in Sarnath, Lumbini Grove in Nepal, Adam's Peak in Sri Lanka, and the Palace of the Dalai Lama in Tibet.
7. Buddhists strive to embody compassion, inner peace, and right action.

Page 47

1. Someone born in 1760 BCE is older.
2. The difference is 500 years.
3. The difference is 2,960 years.
4. Answers will vary. One possibility is 1450-1550.
5. It is the 21st century.